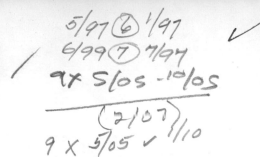

TAJIKISTAN

TAJIKISTAN

THEN & NOW

Prepared by
Geography Department

Lerner Publications Company
Minneapolis

Series editors: Mary M. Rodgers, Tom Streissguth,
  Colleen Sexton
Photo researcher: Kathy Raskob
Designer: Zachary Marell

Our thanks to the following for their help in preparing
and checking the text of this book: Dr. Craig ZumBrunnen,
Department of Geography, University of Washington;
Vikki Shane, Department of Uralic and Altaic Studies,
Indiana University.

Terms in **bold** appear in a glossary that starts on page 52.

Pronunciation Guide

Dushanbe	dyoo-SHAHN-buh
Genghis	GEN-giss
glasnost	GLAZ-nost
Kakhar Makhkamov	kah-CAR mah-KAH-mov
Khojent	koh-JENT
Khiva	KEE-vuh
Kulyab	kuhl-YAAB
Kyrgyzstan	keer-geez-STAHN
perestroika	pehr-eh-STROY-kah
Rakhmon Nabiyev	rahk-MAHN nah-BEE-yev
Shiite	SHEE-Iyt
Ura-Tyube	oor-uh—tyoo-BAY
Uzbekistan	ooz-bek-ih-STAHN

LIBRARY OF CONGRESS CATALOGING-IN-PUBLICATION DATA

   Tajikistan / prepared by Geography Department, Lerner Publica-
tions Company.
      p.   cm.—(Then & now)
   Includes index.
   Summary: Discusses the geography, history, people, economics,
politics, and future of the central Asian country that was the
poorest Soviet republic.
   ISBN 0-8225-2816-9 (lib. bdg.)
   1. Tajikistan—Juvenile literature. [1. Tajikistan.] I. Lerner
Publications Company. Geography Dept. II. Series: Then & now
(Minneapolis, Minn.)
DK923.T368 1993
958'.6—dc20   92-40237
                                                    CIP
                                                     AC

• CONTENTS •

According to tradition, young, unmarried Tajik women wear many braids in their hair.

"You can't separate something religious from something national."
Qadi Haji Akbar Turadzhonzoda
Islamic Leader of Tajikistan

In 1992, the Soviet Union would have celebrated the 75th anniversary of the revolution of 1917. During that revolt, political activists called **Communists** overthrew the czar (ruler) and the government of the **Russian Empire.** The revolution of 1917 was the first step in establishing the 15-member **Union of Soviet Socialist Republics (USSR).**

The Soviet Union stretched from eastern Europe across northern Asia and contained nearly 300 million people. Within this vast nation, the Communist government guaranteed housing, education, health care, and lifetime employment. Communist leaders told farmers and factory workers that Soviet citizens owned all property in common. The new nation quickly **industrialized,** meaning it built many new factories and upgraded existing ones. It also modernized and enlarged its farms. In addition, the USSR created a huge, well-equipped military force that allowed it to become one of the most powerful nations in the world.

In Dushanbe, the capital of Tajikistan, a family gathers to eat its evening meal, which includes cucumbers, strawberries, nuts, and thick, round loaves of bread.

By the early 1990s, the Soviet Union was in a period of rapid change and turmoil. The central government had mismanaged the economy, which was failing to provide goods. To control the various ethnic groups within the USSR, the Communists had long restricted many freedoms. People throughout the vast nation were dissatisfied.

Tajikistan, located in distant central Asia, shared many of the problems of the other Soviet republics, including inadequate housing, rising unemployment, and severe poverty. These concerns had sparked unrest in Dushanbe, the Tajik capital city.

Several of the republics were seeking independence from Soviet rule—a development that worried some old-style Communists. In August 1991, these conservative Communists tried to use Soviet military power to overthrow the nation's president. Their effort failed and hastened the breakup of the USSR.

Tajikistan proclaimed its independence from Soviet rule in September 1991, but political instability followed the declaration. Pro-Communist and pro-democratic factions have separately seized the government, ousting the president and calling for reform. Fighting has broken out in parts of the country that are struggling to survive the collapse of the state-controlled economy. Food and energy shortages are common, and housing is still unavailable for many Tajiks. These problems have forced many people from their homes. A large number of the refugees have fled to neighboring Afghanistan.

Civil war rocked Tajikistan during the early 1990s. Here, soldiers patrol the streets of Dushanbe, where groups in favor of democratic ideas compete for power with people who support the old Communist ways.

In Panjikent, a small city in western Tajikistan, boys exercise on a jungle gym.

Amid this turmoil there has been a revival of the religion of Islam, which the Soviets had severely restricted. Members of Islamic political parties are demanding that Islamic principles guide Tajikistan's new administration, and people are relearning the faith's ancient prayers and laws. Hopes for progress will fade, however, if Tajiks cannot achieve stable government.

Most Tajiks follow the religion of Islam, which was introduced to the region in the 8th century A.D. Islamic believers, called Muslims, pray five times each day while kneeling in the direction of Mecca, a Middle Eastern city that is the center of Islam.

CHAPTER ONE

The Land and People of Tajikistan

A landlocked country in the center of Asia, Tajikistan covers 55,250 square miles (143,100 square kilometers)—an area about the size of Greece or the state of Wisconsin. China borders Tajikistan in the east, and Afghanistan lies in the south. China and Afghanistan have large populations of Tajiks, the main ethnic group of Tajikistan.

Two former Soviet republics also share boundaries with Tajikistan. Uzbekistan is in the west and north, and Kyrgyzstan sits in the northeast. The Soviet government drew borders in the area with little regard for the wishes of the people in the region. As a result, Tajiks, Uzbeks, and Kyrgyz all claim parts of one another's territories.

A rural woman and her son enjoy a morning laugh near their home in the Hissar-Alai Mountains. More than two-thirds of Tajikistan's 5.5 million people live in small villages called **qishlaqs.**

Tajikistan has five distinct regions, which are named after major cities and which differ politically. Khojent (formerly Leninabad), in the northwest, is an industrial hub where support for the old Communist system is strong. Kulyab, along the border with Afghanistan, also backs traditional Soviet policies. Surrounding Dushanbe are groups that endorse a coalition of democratic and Communist leaders. In the southwest is Kurgan-Tyube, a democratic stronghold. The people of Gorno-Badakhshan, a mountainous region in eastern Tajikistan, have close ties to the Islamic movement.

(Left) **An aerial view shows a settlement in southern Tajikistan that lies in the foothills of the mountains.** *(Above)* **Carrying water from a stream or other source to the family home is part of everyday life in Tajik qishlaqs.**

• The Lay of the Land •

With high, rugged mountains and deep, fertile valleys, Tajikistan is a land of contrasts. More than 90 percent of the nation lies at least 10,000 feet (3,048 meters) above sea level, but about 80 percent of Tajiks live at elevations of less than 3,281 feet (1,000 m). Most people dwell in small villages, called **qishlaqs,** in the valleys or near water sources. Tajikistan, which lies in a geologically unstable area, is also prone to earthquakes.

Several mountain systems cross Tajikistan. The Tien Mountains rise in the north. The Turkestan, Zeravshan, and Hissar-Alai ranges dominate the northwestern part of the country. The Pamir Mountains, which contain the highest peaks of the former Soviet Union, are located in the southeast. Summits in Gorno-Badakhshan reach heights of more than 23,000 feet (7,010 m) above sea level.

Glaciers, slow-moving masses of ice that date from hundreds of thousands of years ago, are common at high elevations in Tajikistan. The Fedchenko Glacier, one of the longest glaciers in the world, stretches 44 miles (71 km) in Gorno-Badakhshan. Melting glacial ice feeds streams that irrigate farmland in the country's dry basins and valleys.

Most of Tajikistan's 5.5 million people live in one of three major river valleys. The Fergana Valley, which stretches into Uzbekistan, lies in the north and supports productive farms. The Hissar and Vakhsh valleys—where Tajiks and Kyrgyz raise livestock—dominate the west central and southwestern regions, respectively.

The long, wide Fedchenko Glacier (mass of slow-moving ice) passes through the Pamir Mountains of southeastern Tajikistan.

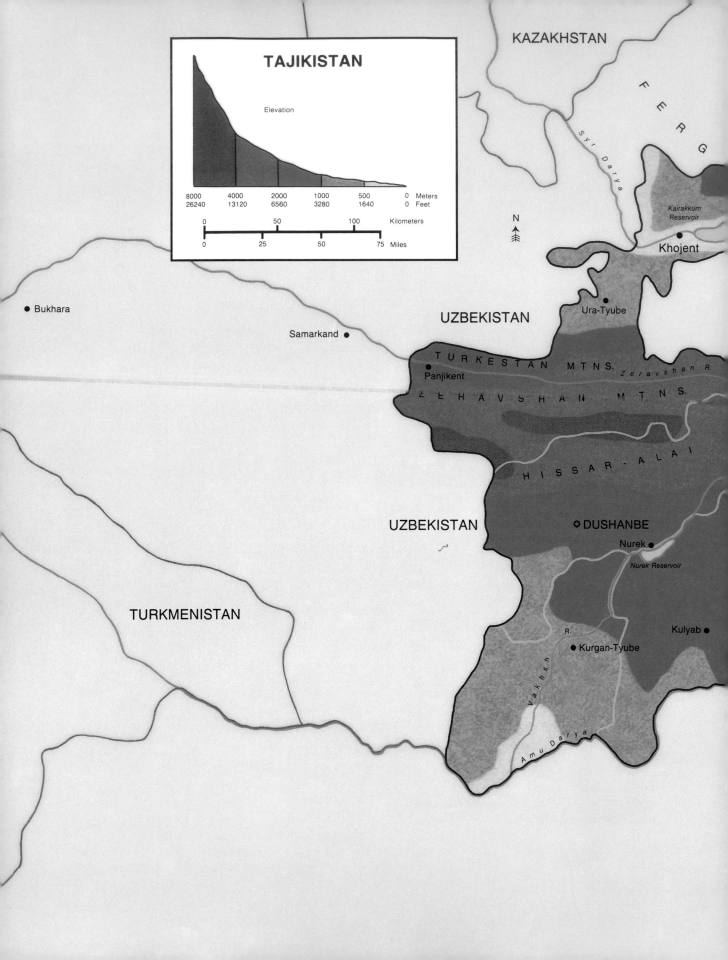

TAJIKISTAN

Elevation

| 8000 | 4000 | 2000 | 1000 | 500 | 0 | Meters |
| 26240 | 13120 | 6560 | 3280 | 1640 | 0 | Feet |

| 0 | | 50 | | 100 | | Kilometers |
| 0 | 25 | | 50 | | 75 | Miles |

KAZAKHSTAN

F E R G

N

● Bukhara

Samarkand ●

UZBEKISTAN

Syr Darya

Kairakkum
Reservoir

● Khojent

Ura-Tyube ●

T U R K E S T A N   M T N S.

Panjikent
●

Zeravshan R.

Z E R A V S H A N   M T N S.

H I S S A R - A L A I

UZBEKISTAN

⊕ DUSHANBE

Nurek ●

Nurek Reservoir

TURKMENISTAN

Kulyab ●

R.

● Kurgan-Tyube

Vakhsh

Amu Darya

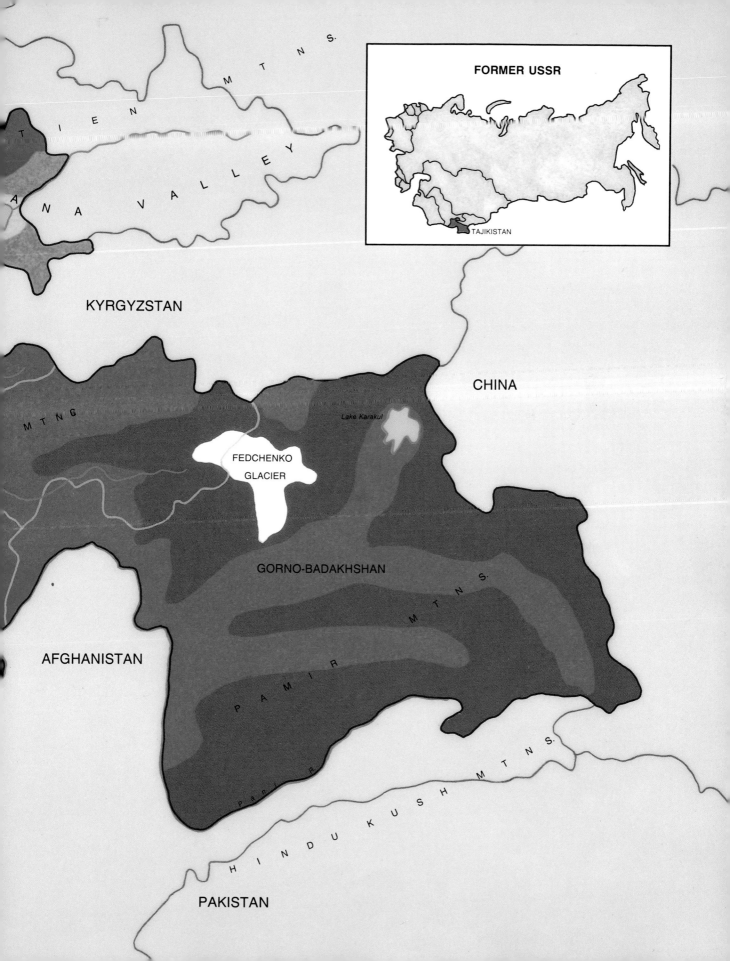

FORMER USSR

TAJIKISTAN

TIEN MTNS.

T
I
E   VALLEY
N

A   N   A

KYRGYZSTAN

CHINA

MTN G

Lake Karakul

FEDCHENKO
GLACIER

GORNO-BADAKHSHAN

P
A
M
I
R
  M T N S.

AFGHANISTAN

Panj R.

H I N D U K U S H   M T N S.

PAKISTAN

• Waterways and Climate •

Tajikistan's rivers, most of which flow westward from the mountains, irrigate farmland and power hydroelectric stations. The country's main waterways are the Amu Darya, the Syr Darya, and the Zeravshan River. (*Darya* means "river" in Persian.) In addition, Tajikistan has more than 500 mountain streams, many of which are dammed to create hydroelectric power.

Lake Karakul, Tajikistan's largest body of water, covers 141 square miles (365 square km) in the mountainous northeast. Lying more than 2 miles (3 km) above sea level, the lake is 780 feet (238 m) deep. Experts believe the salty, lifeless lake was formed when a huge meteorite hit the region millions of years ago. The Kairakkum Reservoir, which is also called the Tajik Sea, is a large artificial lake near Khojent. Water from this reservoir and from the Nurek Reservoir farther south irrigate land and generate electricity.

People in Tajikistan experience very cold winters and hot summers. The average temperature in

The Zeravshan River (above) *begins in the Hissar-Alai Mountains of northwestern Tajikistan and flows northward to cities in neighboring Uzbekistan. Scientists believe that the impact of a meteorite formed the basin of Lake Karakul* (below).

Only hardy plants, such as this thistle, can grow naturally in Tajikistan's dry climate.

Wearing brightly colored silk dresses, women do their daily shopping in Dushanbe.

January, the coldest month, ranges from 36°F (2°C) in the valleys to –4°F (–20°C) in the Pamirs. In July, the hottest month, average readings are 86°F (30°C) in the valleys and 32°F (0°C) in the Pamirs. Because Tajikistan is landlocked, it receives very little precipitation. In some mountainous areas, as little as 3 inches (8 centimeters) fall per year.

In the summer, strong winds roar through the mountain valleys of Tajikistan. The **garmsir** (the Persian word for "hot place") is a very hot, dry wind that blows from the south. This wind brings a sudden rise in temperature that can dry out crops or can ripen them too early. The **afghanets** (the Russian word for "Afghan") arrives from the southwest and carries dust and dirt. To avoid the dry, gritty blasts, Tajiks cover their faces when they are outside.

• Cities •

Only about 30 percent of Tajikistan's population live in urban areas. Some of the country's cities once welcomed merchants and travelers who were following the historic Silk Road that passed through central Asia 2,000 years ago. Other cities have developed only since the 19th and 20th centuries.

The country's capital, Dushanbe (population 604,000), is an industrial and cultural hub in western Tajikistan. Before the Soviets took over in the early 20th century, Dushanbe was a village of a few hundred people. The Soviets made it the Tajik capital in 1929 and renamed the city Stalinabad, after the Soviet leader Joseph Stalin. By 1961, however, Stalin was dead and in disgrace, and Dushanbe regained its pre-Soviet name. In recent times, Dushanbe has been the scene of ethnic rioting and political protests, most of which take place in front of imposing government buildings that were constructed during the Soviet era.

Factories in Dushanbe process meat, cotton, and silk and make refrigerators, furniture, cement, farm machinery, and leather goods. Dushanbe is also the country's educational center. The Tajik Academy of Sciences, Tajik University, and other institutions of higher learning attract many students, professors, and scientists.

The 2,500-year-old city of Khojent (population 169,000) is located in the Fergana Valley. Khojent has long been an important commercial hub that attracted many invaders. The Greek king Alexander the Great arrived in 330 B.C., and Arab armies plundered the city in the 8th century A.D. Central Asian Mongols completely destroyed Khojent in 1220. The Russians captured the city in 1866. Under Soviet rule, Khojent became a major center for the production of silk, footwear, and clothing.

The modern city of Panjikent (population 51,000) is located in the Zeravshan Valley near the ruins of ancient Panjikent, which existed from the 5th to the 8th centuries A.D. Modern Panjikent's most important industrial enterprises include a cannery, a meat-packaging plant, a dairy, a brickyard, and a winery. Ura-Tyube in northwestern Tajikistan and Kurgan-Tyube and Kulyab in the southwest are other cities that support both agricultural and industrial businesses.

• Ethnic Heritage •

Ethnic Tajiks have been living in central Asia since at least the 6th century B.C. and now make up 62 percent of the population of Tajikistan. They are descended from Persian (modern Iranian) peoples who spoke a language related to Persian, the language of Iran. A very small subgroup of the Tajiks are the Pamiris, who live mostly in the Pamir Mountains.

(Above) *A view through an archway in Khojent (formerly Leninabad) reveals some of the historic buildings in this 2,500-year-old city in northern Tajikistan.* (Below) *In Ura-Tyube, an industrial town in northwestern Tajikistan, a woman sells homemade bread from a street cart.*

White-roofed houses dominate the skyline of modern Panjikent. The city lies near the ruins of ancient Panjikent, which was a cultural and trading hub until Arab armies destroyed it in the 8th century A.D.

They speak a slightly different form of Persian and follow a different branch of the Islamic religion. About one million Tajiks live in neighboring Uzbekistan.

Turkic peoples moved into the area in the 6th century A.D. Among the Turkic-speaking groups are **ethnic Uzbeks,** who make up about 24 percent of the nation's population. The country also has small numbers of Kyrgyz, Turkmen, and Kazakhs—Turkic peoples who come from other former Soviet republics in central Asia.

In the late 19th century, Russians settled in Tajikistan's cities and mixed little with the Tajik and Turkic populations. Although only about 8 percent of the country's total population are **ethnic Russians,** they form the majority of the country's skilled laborers and managers. Since independence, many Russians have emigrated because they fear that new government policies will cost them their jobs. Small numbers of Tatars, Ukrainians, and Germans complete the country's ethnic mixture.

(Left) *For the wedding of his granddaughter, an ethnic Tajik wears a traditional turban, robe, and dagger.* (Above) *Russian and Tajik children bask in the sunshine after a summer swim.*

• Health and Education •

Like its central Asian neighbors, Tajikistan has a high birthrate. In fact, the country has the fastest growing population among former Soviet republics. If current trends continue, the population of 5.5 million could double in 22 years. Tajik women have an average of five children during their lifetimes. Large families are especially common in rural areas, where many young people are unemployed. The rapid population growth is also causing an uneven distribution of people among the country's age groups. Half the population is less than 20 years of age, and one-third are 9 or younger.

The Soviet regime improved the quality and availability of medical care, which has helped Tajiks to live longer than ever before. Life expectancy is 70 years, and 4 percent of the population is older than 65. Although the birthrate is high, the infant mortality rate is also high. Among former Soviet republics, Tajikistan has the second worst infant death rate—73 deaths in every 1,000 live births. Only Turkmenistan's is higher.

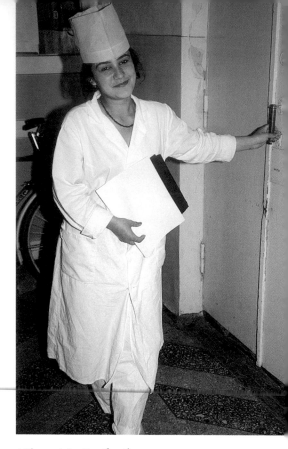

(Above) **In Dushanbe, a nurse prepares to enter a hospital's X-ray room.** (Below) **Boys gather in a playground in Panjikent. About one-third of Tajikistan's population is younger than nine years of age.**

GROWING PAINS IN TAJIKISTAN

Among former Soviet republics, Tajikistan has the highest population growth rate—3.2 percent. At this rate, the nation's population of 5.5 million will double in just 22 years. Several other states in central Asia—including Uzbekistan, Kyrgyzstan, and Turkmenistan—also are growing at a fast pace.

Rapid population growth is affecting Tajikistan's natural environment. As the population rises, for example, Tajiks must expand farmland to produce more food crops. This expansion intensifies the pressure on central Asia's river-fed irrigation systems, which are needed to ripen crops. In a year, central Asian farmers drain off all but 38,846 cubic feet (1,100 cubic meters) of the area's riverwater. Rainfall and melting snow replace some—but not all—of this precious resource.

In addition to making more demands on available water resources, the growing population also creates the potential for conflict. Tajikistan must share the water in central Asia with Uzbekistan, Kyrgyzstan, and Turkmenistan. Unless they can cooperate now on fair use and on conservation measures, these new states may be competing for even less food and water in the coming decades.

During their child-bearing years (roughly 15 to 49), Tajik women have an average of five children.

Finding safe water for cooking, cleaning, and bathing is a daily chore in Tajikistan. This young girl is washing at a public tap, where people come to fill large containers with water.

Patrons study in one of eight reading rooms in Dushanbe's main library. The building, which holds more than three million books, is named after the Tajik poet and historian Abu al-Qasem Mansur Firdawsi, who lived in the 10th and 11th centuries. Roughly 500 people use the library every day.

Currently, the old Soviet educational system is still in place. Although preschools exist, most children are kept at home until they begin primary school at the age of seven. Primary school usually takes nine years to complete, and secondary school lasts for two or three years. Some students choose to attend a vocational school, which provides both a secondary education and job training.

More than 65,000 students attend Tajikistan's postsecondary schools. Although Tajik University in Dushanbe is the major institution of higher learning, several other medical, agricultural, educational,

Until the 20th century, the Tajik language was written in the Arabic alphabet, in which ornate copies of Tajik poetry and philosophy appear.

and arts schools exist throughout the country. A new university was founded in Khojent in 1991.

• *Language* •

Under Soviet rule, Tajik, Uzbek, and Russian were the official languages of Tajikistan. Russian was used mainly in the cities, where Russians worked in industry and government. The Soviets made fluency in Russian a requirement for promotion. Lack of interest and inadequate instruction kept many ethnic Tajiks from learning Russian well. As a result, few ethnic Tajiks attained upper-level jobs in business or government.

The Tajik language, including the dialect spoken by the Pamiris, belongs to the Iranian family of languages and is similar to modern Persian. In July 1989, Tajik became the country's official language. Since most Russians in Tajikistan have chosen not to learn Tajik, many of them now fear they will lose their jobs.

Originally written in Arabic letters, Tajik has appeared in two other alphabets in the 20th century. In 1928, the Soviets adopted the Latin alphabet for Tajik. At about the same time, Turkey chose the Latin alphabet, in which English is written, for Turkish. In 1940, to discourage links between Turkey and Tajikistan, Soviet leaders then ordered that Tajik be written in Cyrillic, the alphabet in which Russian and other Slavic languages appear.

Tajikistan will probably discontinue using Cyrillic but has yet to decide whether to adopt Arabic or Latin lettering. Tajikistan was the first central Asian republic to teach the Arabic script in a literary journal, and many Tajik publications have begun to appear in Arabic. Economic ties with Turkey and Europe, however, may encourage Tajik leaders to choose the Latin alphabet.

• *Religion and Festivals* •

Until the Arab conquest of the 8th century A.D., Tajiks followed many religions. The Arabs converted the Tajiks to Islam, a faith that eventually split into Sunni and Shiite branches. Most Tajiks follow the majority Sunni form of Islam. The Pamiris, however, are Ismailis—a separate sect of the Shiite branch.

Muslims (followers of Islam) have several religious duties, including daily prayer, occasional fasting, and aid to the poor. Some Tajik Muslims want Tajikistan's new government to adopt **Sharia**, the code of laws based on the Koran (the Islamic holy book).

Under Soviet rule, all religious practices were greatly discouraged. The Communists closed Islamic schools and mosques (houses of prayer) and persecuted Islamic leaders. Nevertheless, believers continued to observe fasts and holidays, to visit the tombs of saints, and to participate in rituals related to birth, marriage, and death.

Long horns are a feature of joyful Tajik occasions, including weddings, births, and homecomings. Here, musicians welcome a passenger at Dushanbe's airport.

(Right) **As part of the ritual of circumcision, Tajik boys put on embroidered robes and special skullcaps. The ritual, which involves cutting a fold of skin, is an age-old part of Tajik culture.** (Below) **Dushanbe's main mosque (Islamic house of prayer) has been an educational center, as well as a hub of the Islamic political movement in Tajikistan.**

Since independence, the government has lifted most restrictions on religion. Muslims freely observe the Feast of Sacrifice and officially celebrate the ending of the month-long fast that is part of Ramadan. Workers are restoring mosques, and Islamic schools have reopened.

Although most of Tajikistan's citizens are Muslims, other religions are practiced. Russian settlers brought the Orthodox form of Christianity, which some Ukrainians also follow. Other Ukrainians belong to the Ukrainian Catholic Church. Most Germans in Tajikistan are members of the Lutheran Church, a Protestant Christian sect.

CHAPTER TWO

Tajikistan's Story

Despite its isolated location, Tajikistan has a rich and varied cultural heritage. Caravan routes that passed through the country attracted merchants from Europe, pilgrims from China, and missionaries from Persia. Foreigners who arrived by the trade routes brought new religions, as well as new styles of art, literature, and architecture. Tajikistan also suffered military invasions from Europe and Asia, events that introduced foreign ethnic groups and languages.

• The Pre-Islamic Era •

Archaeological evidence shows that prehistoric people lived in Tajikistan almost 200,000 years ago. The Elamites, who built settlements in the mountain valleys, moved into the region in about 3000 B.C. Within a thousand years, other groups, including the Persians, had set up provinces and kingdoms in Tajikistan.

The Hissar Fortress, located about 19 miles (30 kilometers) south of the capital, was the summer home of the khans (princes) of Bukhara. They controlled Tajikistan from the 16th to the 19th centuries.

This silver coin dates from 323 B.C., the year that Alexander the Great died. It depicts Zeus, the most powerful of the Greek gods, sitting on a throne holding an eagle. The Greek lettering translates as "Alexander the king." Alexander's empire, which included Tajikistan, broke up after his death.

From the 6th to the 4th centuries B.C., Tajikistan was under the rule of the Persian Achaemenid dynasty (family of rulers). The Achaemenids used local leaders, called **satraps**, to administer each **satrapy.** To promote trade, the Achaemenids built roads, and Persian missionaries spread the **Zoroastrian** religion.

The Achaemenids were overthrown by the Greek armies of Alexander the Great, who invaded central Asia in 330 B.C. Alexander conquered prosperous trading centers, including Khojent, and introduced Greek art and culture to the region. Alexander's goal was to merge the Greek and Persian states into a single superpower. His death in 323 B.C., however, foiled this plan. Alexander's large empire was then divided among four of his generals, one of whom—Seleucus—got the section that included Tajikistan.

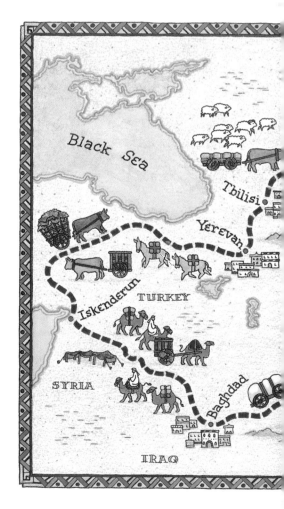

Passing through central Asia, the Silk Road linked China to the Middle East and Europe. Caravans brought bolts of fine silk fabric westward, while wool, gold, silver, horses, wine, and other merchandise made the journey eastward. Few merchants traveled the entire route. Instead, goods moved from city to city with the help of local brokers. Depending on the terrain and the weather, caravan drivers used camels, donkeys, oxen, or horses for transport.

Frequent foreign attacks brought down the Seleucid kingdom after only a few centuries. By about the 1st century A.D., the Kushan people of the Hindu Kush Mountains of northern Afghanistan were occupying Tajikistan. Kushan kings, who followed the faith of Buddhism, spread its message of peace and religious tolerance to the peoples of Tajikistan.

The Kushan Empire's economy depended on trade and on the profits from overland caravan routes between southern Europe, the Middle East, and eastern Asia. For several hundred years, Tajikistan benefited from Kushan control. The building

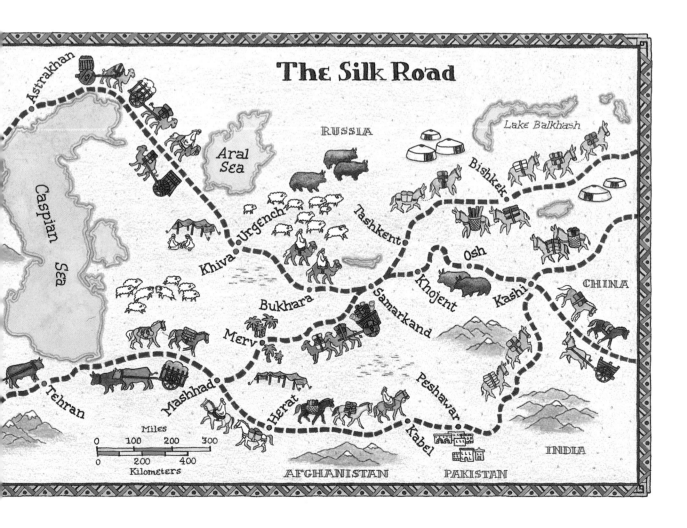

of extensive irrigation canals, for example, allowed farmers to grow an abundance of crops. Traditional art and handicrafts flourished, and trade expanded. Cities increased in size, with Panjikent becoming one of the most prominent cultural hubs of central Asia.

This peaceful existence was shattered by an invasion of nomadic Turks in the 6th century A.D. Arriving from the northeast, they quickly took control of most of Kushan's cities and caravan routes. The Turks slowly abandoned their nomadic lifestyles and settled in Tajikistan as farmers and merchants.

• The Coming of Islam •

Another invasion occurred in the 8th century A.D., when Arab armies from the Middle East crossed the Amu Darya and conquered central Asia. The Arabs, who followed the religion of Islam, met strong resistance to their attempts to convert the region's people. During their campaign, the Arabs destroyed Panjikent, as well as Bukhara and Samarkand (cities now in Uzbekistan). Eventually, the various religions in Tajikistan gave way to the Islamic faith.

The vast Arab Empire, which stretched from North Africa to India, was too big to govern without the help of local leaders. In the 9th century, Samankhoda, a Persian noble who was allied with the Arabs, founded the Samanid dynasty with Bukhara as its capital. Under Samanid rule, mining and farming greatly increased in Tajikistan. As the Persian and central Asian cultures merged, Bukhara became a major center of Tajik art and learning. Tajik-Persian language and literature spread throughout central Asia. Stability in the region allowed trade to flourish. The busy caravan routes carried goods to areas as distant as the Baltic coast—roughly 2,500 miles (4,023 km) to the northwest.

A memorial statue of Abu Abdollah Rudaki stands in a Dushanbe park. Born near ancient Panjikent, Rudaki became the court poet to the Samanid rulers in the 10th century. He wrote thousands of poems—about 1,000 of which are preserved—that praise bravery, love, truth, and reason.

Samarkand, now in Uzbekistan, was the center of Tajik-Persian culture and education in the Samanid era. An aerial view of the city's skyline shows the domes and towers of many historic buildings.

Turkic invasions caused Samanid power to wane at the end of the 10th century. From the 11th to the 13th centuries, Tajikistan was ruled by Turkic dynasties that frequently warred among themselves. Despite these conflicts, Tajik cities continued to expand and prosper from the mining of gold and other precious metals. During this period, Persian missionaries introduced the Ismaili form of Shiite Islam to the Pamiris. Islam remained the dominant cultural force in the region, and Tajik authors penned major works on Islamic philosophy and law.

By the early 1200s, the peoples of Tajikistan—especially those living in the valleys of the Syr Darya and the Amu Darya—were becoming slowly **Turkized.** They continued to follow the Islamic religion but were influenced by the language and culture of their Turkic rulers. The dialect of Persian spoken in the region, for example, borrowed many words from Turkish.

• New Conquerors •

In the 13th century, the peoples of central Asia experienced a destructive invasion. Under the leadership of Genghis Khan, a huge army of Mongol warriors attacked the area in the 1220s. After leveling Khojent, the Mongols massacred the city's population and demolished surrounding farms and irrigation works. Only the most unreachable mountain valleys of the Pamirs escaped destruction. The Mongols conquered a huge realm that covered central Asia and eastern Europe. After the death of Genghis Khan, however, the Mongol Empire began to split apart.

Timur—one of Genghis's descendants (whom Europeans called Tamerlane)—revived the Mongol Empire in the 14th century. With his armies of Turks and of Turkic-speaking Mongols, he conquered vast amounts of territory between the Black Sea in the west and India in the east.

After Timur's death in 1405, Mongol power declined in Tajikistan as other groups fought for control of the region. In the early 16th century, the Turkic-speaking Uzbeks conquered central Asia under the leadership of Muhammad Shaybani. From this time onward, Uzbeks and Tajiks became ethnically mixed. Members of these groups, especially those living in urban areas, learned to speak both Tajik and Uzbek.

Overland trade was still an essential part of central Asia's economy. In the 1500s, when European explorers discovered sea routes to Asia, the caravan roads lost importance. Seaborne trade increased, while commerce in central Asia declined. In addition, the region suffered upheaval as conflicts erupted between the Sunni Muslims of Tajikistan and Uzbekistan and the Shiite Muslims of Persia.

These constant wars weakened the Uzbek Empire, which was divided into states called **khanates**,

Born in Samarkand in 1336, the Mongol leader Timur conquered areas far beyond the borders of Uzbekistan and Tajikistan. A skilled but ruthless commander, Timur ordered the slaughter of thousands of people who would not submit to his rule. Yet he supported science and the arts by bringing the finest scholars, poets, and painters to his court.

(Below) *Floral and geometric mosaics are typical designs on Islamic buildings. These artworks decorate a structure in Khiva (now in Uzbekistan), a city whose wealth attracted the armies of the Uzbek and Persian empires.* (Right) *The Uzbek leader Muhammad Shaybani battled the Persians for control of Uzbekistan and Tajikistan in the early 16th century. His success caused Uzbeks and Tajiks to share territory and to learn one another's language. From the 1500s onward, Tajiks and Uzbeks became ethnically mixed. For centuries, they lived in peace under the khans of Bukhara, Khiva, and Kokand.*

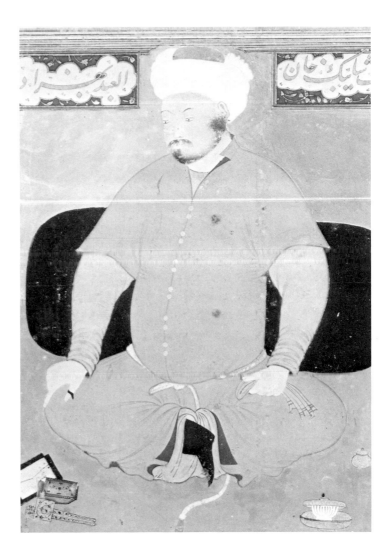

each of which was headed by a **khan** (prince). The khanates of Bukhara and Khiva emerged in the 16th century, and the khanate of Kokand formed in the 18th century. Until the early 1800s, the land of present-day Tajikistan was divided between the Bukharan and the Kokandian khanates.

• Russian Conquest •

Frequent wars among the khanates hampered their ability to fend off foreign powers—including the British in Afghanistan to the south and the Russian Empire to the north. The British were trying to take over Afghanistan, while the Russians were pushing into central Asia. By the mid-19th century, Tajikistan and Afghanistan were caught between the territorial claims of two world powers.

With its well-equipped armies, Russia invaded the Bukharan khanate in 1866 and seized Khojent. Two years later, the Russian czar (ruler) made Bukhara a **protectorate**, meaning the empire pledged to safeguard the khanate from attack but did not dismantle it. The central and southwestern sections of modern Tajikistan, along with the western Pamirs, remained part of the Bukharan protectorate.

The Russians absorbed Khiva in 1873 and abolished Kokand in 1876. Khiva became a protectorate. Kokand, which included northern Tajikistan and eastern Uzbekistan, was added to the territory of **Russian Turkestan**, an administrative unit of the Russian Empire. Under an agreement between Russia and Britain in 1895, Russia gained control of the lands north of the Panj River and of the western Pamirs. To the south of these border markers lay Afghanistan, which was home to a large number of ethnic Tajiks.

Russian rule brought economic changes to Tajikistan. The Russians established huge cotton plantations to supply a growing international demand for cotton fiber. New factories in the region processed cotton and other agricultural products, including rice, sugar beets, and grapes. The Russians also constructed railroads to ease the export of cotton and the import of fabrics and china.

Very little cultural change took place in Tajikistan, however. Schools were founded, but few Tajik children attended them. Large numbers of Russians moved into Tajikistan's cities, but most Tajiks con-

(Below) **Round towers domi-nate the main gates of the Hissar Fortress. During the hot summer months, the khans of Bukhara retreated to this mountain stronghold to enjoy its cool mountain air and sur-rounding natural beauty. (Right) A 19th-century cartoon portrays the British Empire's lion holding back the Russian Empire's bear, as both gaze hungrily at central Asia.**

tinued to live in qishlaqs, where traditional family life and religious practices remained undisturbed.

• Soviet Tajikistan •

In the early 20th century, Tajiks and other central Asians began to resist Russian domination of their lands. In addition, Russia was drafting Tajiks to work and fight in World War I (1914–1918), an international conflict that pitted Russia and its allies against Germany, Austria, and Turkey. To feed and clothe the Russian army, the government increased exports of central Asian cotton and cut back on deliveries of grain and other foods. The discontent worsened in 1916, when the shortage of food—along with a large crop failure—triggered famine. Revolts against oppressive czarist rule erupted throughout Turkestan.

The war's hardships were also causing turmoil in other parts of the Russian Empire. In 1917, Russian political activists called Communists led a revolution that promised workers better wages,

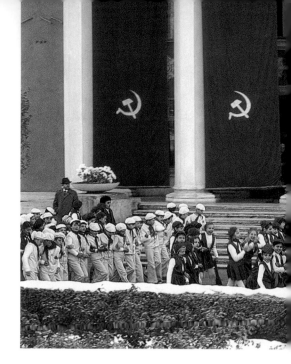

more food, and peace. After toppling the czar, the revolution spread to Turkestan. The Communists took power in northern Tajikistan in 1918 and made the area part of the **Turkestan Autonomous Soviet Socialist Republic.** Nevertheless, many Tajiks opposed Communist rule and demanded independence.

By 1921, the remainder of Tajikistan, which had belonged to the Bukharan protectorate, was conquered by the Communist Red Army. Much of this land was included in the newly formed **People's Republic of Bukhara.** A year later, the Communists established the Union of Soviet Socialist Republics (USSR).

Meanwhile, the USSR rejected Tajik demands for self-rule, an action that fostered an armed, anti-Soviet revolt known as the Basmachi movement. The rebel leader Ibrahim Bek spearheaded the rebellion, which continued until 1926, when the Red Army brought Turkestan under its control.

In 1924, the Soviet government began the **delimitation** of Russian Turkestan. This process drew new borders that created five central Asian Soviet Socialist Republics (SSRs). At first, Tajikistan was included in the Uzbek SSR. But by 1929, the Soviets had established the Tajik SSR as a full member of the larger USSR. The delimitation also split the fertile Fergana Valley between Uzbekistan and Tajikistan.

• *World War II and Its Aftermath* •

In the 1930s and 1940s, the Soviets increased the production of cotton in Tajikistan by forcing Tajiks who lived in mountainous regions to move into valleys where cotton could be planted. The Soviets then took over small, private farms, combining them into large, state-owned **collective farms** that

A statue in Khojent commemorates Tajik soldiers who died fighting against the Germans in World War II (1939–1945).

(Above) **Under Soviet rule, children in Dushanbe prepared to participate in May Day celebrations that honored the workers of the world.** (Below) **A statue of Vladimir Lenin, the founder of the Soviet state, towers above the main square of Nurek, a city famous for the huge hydroelectric station that is located nearby.**

could grow vast amounts of cotton. Many of the people who resisted collectivization were killed or imprisoned.

Food and textiles from Tajikistan benefited the USSR during World War II (1939–1945), when much of the western part of the Soviet Union was under siege. In the postwar decades, the Soviets developed heavy industries in Tajikistan to make autos, refrigerators, and farm machinery. On the social level, the government expanded education, a policy that by the 1980s had raised the literacy rate for Tajikistan to 98 percent.

Soviet rule did not benefit all Soviet citizens equally. Some regions of the USSR received more investment than others. Tajikistan, a small republic with few resources and a high birthrate, was among the poorest members of the Soviet Union. Lack of housing, high unemployment, and extreme poverty plagued the population. Yet strict Soviet control of the media and of the economy allowed little social criticism or economic reform.

Tajikistan's problems were discussed more freely after Mikhail Gorbachev became the leader of the USSR in 1985. His policy of **glasnost**, or "openness," encouraged Tajik citizens to speak out, even if their views were critical of the Soviet government. Another policy, called **perestroika**, aimed to restructure the Soviet economy.

In February 1990, demonstrators gathered in Dushanbe to protest long-neglected economic and social problems. The demonstrations turned into riots, with mobs looting businesses and killing civilians. Tajikistan's Communist party chief, Kakhar Makhkamov, called a state of emergency, and the Soviet army began to patrol the streets. Opposition groups demanded economic and political changes, as well as the resignation of Makhkamov and other Communist leaders in Tajikistan.

In late 1992, in Dushanbe, the flag (right) *of the independent republic of Tajikistan flew above the parliament building, which has been the scene of many demonstrations for independence and reform* (below). **Some of the protests in the central square have led to riots and to the removal of governmental leaders.**

• Recent Events •

The unrest in Tajikistan mirrored the events in other parts of the USSR in the early 1990s. Many republics were declaring self-rule over their political and economic activities. Conservative Communist officials, fearing the breakup of the Soviet Union and the loss of their authority, blamed Gorbachev's new policies for the disturbances. To bring the situation under their control, these officials staged a **coup d'état** against Gorbachev on August 19, 1991. At first, President Makhkamov supported the overthrow, saying it would restore order. Under pressure from Tajikistan's opposition groups, however, he later backed Gorbachev.

Within days, the coup had failed, and within weeks all 15 of the Soviet republics had declared their independence. Tajikistan's parliament made the proclamation on September 9 and called for presidential elections. Makhkamov resigned and was replaced by Rakhmon Nabiyev, a former Communist official whom Gorbachev had removed from office for corruption. Elections in November 1991 gave Nabiyev, who comes from northern Tajikistan, nearly 60 percent of the popular vote. In the next month, Tajikistan joined the **Commonwealth of Independent States**, a loose association of former Soviet republics.

The future is uncertain for this young Tajik, whose mountainous country is struggling to establish political and economic stability.

Since independence, various opposition parties have developed in Tajikistan. Among them are Rastokhez (meaning "rebirth"), the Democratic party, and the Islamic Renaissance party. All of these parties want Islamic principles to guide the government, but they do not favor making Tajikistan a strict Islamic state.

Throughout 1992, the political situation in Tajikistan remained tense. In May, anti-government forces gained control of most of the capital city. This action forced Nabiyev to share power with the country's other parties. In September 1992, anti Nabiyev groups surrounded the presidential palace in Dushanbe. This time, they demanded his resignation. They felt Nabiyev had used his office to favor northern Tajikistan and was too slow in making political and economic reforms. For a few months, a coalition of Islamic parties ran the government.

Nabiyev's supporters did not accept his resignation and boycotted the parliament. In October, they staged a coup, occupying legislative and executive buildings. Elections in December 1992 brought pro-Communist leaders to power, but factions continued to fight one another.

Many Tajiks feared that the fighting in the capital would spread to other areas. Clashes had already occurred in Kurgan-Tyube, which supports the democratic movement, and in Kulyab and Khojent, which back former Soviet leaders. Bombs destroyed the only big road linking Khojent and Dushanbe, and the assassination of a senior Tajik politician also increased tensions. An additional issue is the rising number of Tajik refugees who are fleeing their war-torn country for camps in Afghanistan

Tajikistan has a variety of pressing economic and social problems. None of them can be addressed, however, until the civil war—which has already claimed 2,000 lives—ends.

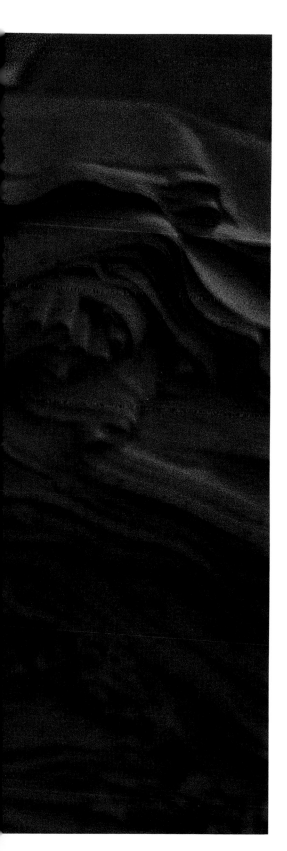

CHAPTER THREE

Making
a Living
in Tajikistan

Even among poor central Asian nations, Tajikistan has a low standard of living. In fact, most experts rank the country as the poorest republic in the old USSR. This status resulted from the Soviet Union's uneven development of Tajikistan's economy. Some areas—such as the Fergana Valley, Khojent, and Dushanbe—received investment, while other regions were largely ignored. Soviet policies also caused social tensions that are still present. Most ethnic Tajiks and ethnic Uzbeks live and work on rural farms, while most Russians operate and manage urban factories.

*A **worker piles up richly dyed fabrics made in a Dushanbe textile mill that employs 10,000 people.***

A cabbage seller proudly holds up her wares at an open-air market.

Although Tajikistan needs to set a new economic course, the nation still uses the Russian ruble as its currency. The Tajik government hopes that this familiar monetary unit will help to stabilize the Tajik economy. But the ruble closely links Tajikistan to Russia's economy, which has severe problems of its own.

Another result of Soviet policies is the wretched state of Tajikistan's environment. Many of the country's farms, factories, and mines pollute the air, water, and soil. Closings or stricter controls of these businesses would benefit environmental conditions. But many people would lose their jobs, and the production of exports would decline. At present, the government is trying to keep farms, factories, and mines open, while looking for cleaner ways to run them.

On a large farm in southwestern Tajikistan, a laborer picks cotton by hand. The country's main crop, cotton supplies raw material to the textile industry.

• Agriculture •

Approximately half of the Tajik population have jobs related to agriculture. The chief crop is cotton, which is planted in the southwest and north. Wheat, barley, vegetables, and melons are cultivated throughout the country. Farmers grow rice on the floodplains of northern and southwestern Tajikistan, as well as in the Zeravshan Valley. Potatoes and tobacco thrive in the foothills and on the lower mountain slopes.

Orchards that produce apples, apricots, peaches, plums, quinces, lemons, pomegranates, and figs exist mainly in northern and southwestern areas of the country. Grape growing is important in southwestern Tajikistan. The grapes are made into wine, which is exported to many countries.

A harvester of tobacco pauses during his work in the mountain foothills.

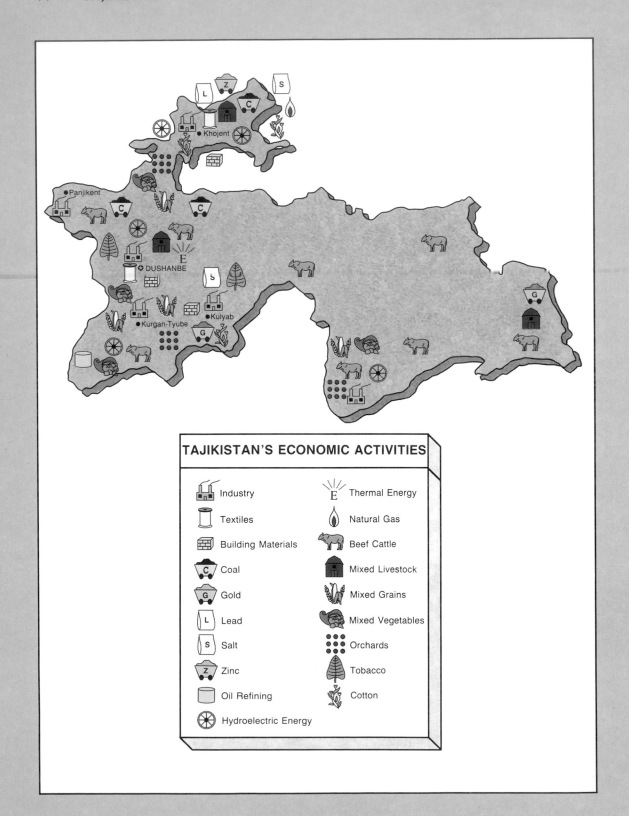

TAJIKISTAN'S ECONOMIC ACTIVITIES

Industry

Textiles

Building Materials

Coal

Gold

Lead

Salt

Zinc

Oil Refining

Hydroelectric Energy

Thermal Energy

Natural Gas

Beef Cattle

Mixed Livestock

Mixed Grains

Mixed Vegetables

Orchards

Tobacco

Cotton

(Above) ***Goats feed on nourishing grasses in the Zeravshan Valley of western Tajikistan.*** (Right) ***Shepherds in search of water and pasture guide their flocks down the rocky slopes of the Pamir Mountains.***

The raising of livestock—chiefly in central and southeastern Tajikistan—is a key branch of Tajik agriculture. The country's rich pastures nourish cattle, sheep, and goats. Farmers raise livestock for their meat, wool, and dairy products. Tajik sheep are bred in the south for their meat, and Karakul sheep produce beautiful, shiny wool. Merchants export Karakul pelts to various countries, where the skins are made into coats, hats, and other items.

The Russians introduced pig farming in the 19th century, but this activity remains a largely Russian occupation. Tajiks do not raise pigs because Islamic customs forbid Muslims to eat pork. Poultry farms exist throughout the country, and dairy farms are especially numerous in the suburban areas of Dushanbe and Khojent. Tajiks and Kyrgyz herd cattle, sheep, and yaks in the eastern Pamirs. Horse breeding remains an important occupation throughout the country.

• Mining and Energy •

About one-third of Tajikistan's population is employed either in mining or processing the country's mineral resources. Workers extract lead and zinc from northern mines and take precious metals, such as gold, from Kulyab and Gorno-Badakhshan. Also in Gorno-Badakhshan lie deposits of salt, rock crystal, asbestos, and semiprecious stones.

Miners dig for coal, the nation's principal fuel, in the north and in the Zeravshan Valley. Southern Tajikistan's deposits of paraffin-rich petroleum, although not suitable for refining into oil, can be processed into asphalt. Pipelines transport natural gas from the Vakhsh and Hissar valleys to Dushanbe. Northern Tajikistan imports natural gas from Uzbekistan.

Tajikistan has built several dams to take advantage of fast-flowing currents on the Vakhsh River and on the Syr Darya. Although these hydroelectric stations are important to the country, they lie in earthquake-prone areas. The earthquakes threaten to crack the dams and to cause floods and mudslides. Plants that run on steam-generated electricity also provide energy to the capital.

(Above) *Water from the Nurek power station on the Vakhsh River irrigates farmland and generates electricity.* (Below) *Among Tajikistan's traditional manufactured goods are household ceramics.*

• Manufacturing and Trade •

For centuries, Tajikistan's economy was based on agriculture, crafts, and trade. These age-old occupations still play an important role. Yet the making of handicrafts—such as pottery, metalware, and carpets—declined in the 20th century, when the Soviets built huge, mass-production factories. Nevertheless, people throughout Tajikistan still supplement their incomes by crafting traditional goods. In addition, many families also raise silkworms, whose cocoons consist of thin fibers that can be processed into silk fabric.

Factories in Dushanbe, Khojent, Kulyab, and Kurgan-Tyube—the country's major industrial centers—produce food, textiles, and leather goods.

(Below) **At a rural market, a Tajik woman offers yellow fruit for sale.** (Bottom) **A Russian factory worker rests beside a mechanized loom.**

Cotton ginning (the process of separating cotton seeds from fiber) and the making of cotton, woolen, and silk textiles are well-developed industries. Carpets, leather goods, and footwear are also manufactured in large quantities. Many of these items are exported to other countries. Tajikistan also manufactures furniture, refrigerators, cables, spare parts for motor vehicles, and agricultural machinery. Building materials—such as cement and concrete—are made in Dushanbe, Khojent, and Kulyab. An aluminum-refining center is also near the capital.

Food processing accounts for one-quarter of the country's total industrial output. Vegetable oil is extracted from cotton and sesame seeds. Plants that package fruits and vegetables are located mainly in the north, and large wineries exist in Dushanbe, Ura-Tyube, and Panjikent. Meat-processing complexes and dairies are also numerous.

Under Soviet rule, Tajikistan sent nearly all of its goods to other parts of the USSR. Trade with foreign nations is a key element of the Tajik government's economic strategy. The country exports foodstuffs to its central Asian neighbors and imports lumber, synthetic fibers, motor vehicles, and engineering equipment.

To promote more trade, Tajikistan has eliminated some commercial restrictions and is strengthening economic ties with Europe, the Middle East, southeastern Asia, and the United States. China, Turkey, Iran, and Pakistan already are establishing regional trade zones that include Tajikistan and the other central Asian republics.

Tajikistan is actively seeking investment from other countries and from the World Bank and the International Monetary Fund. Additional financial assistance may come from membership in other world organizations, such as the **United Nations**, which Tajikistan joined in March 1992.

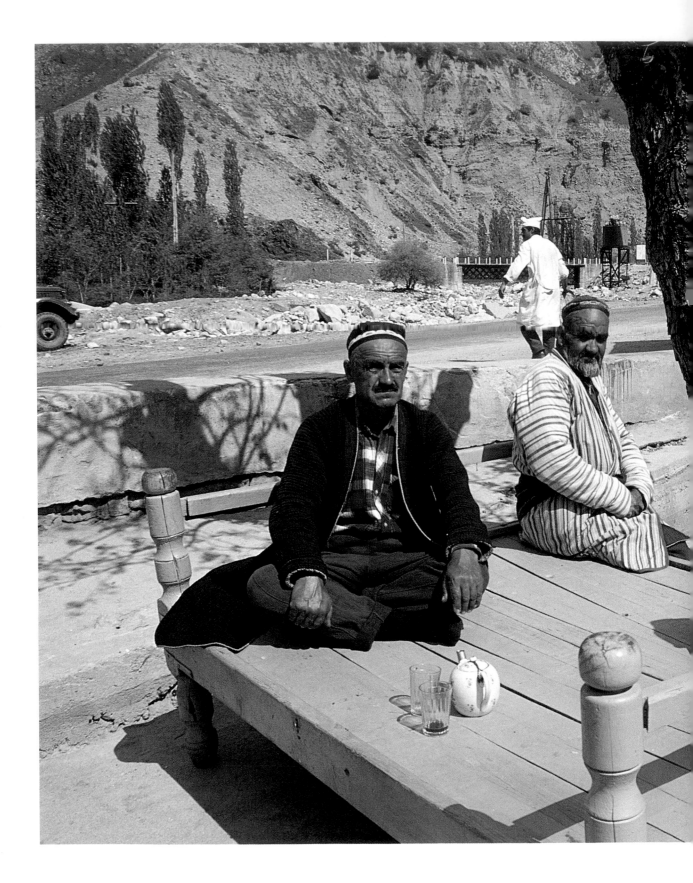

CHAPTER FOUR

What's Next for Tajikistan?

Now that Tajikistan is an independent republic, It must deal with a number of pressing issues, including economic reform and environmental decline. The uncertain political situation, however, limits the government's ability to come up with plans that address these concerns. The factions battling for control of the country must find common ground if progress Is to be made.

Tajiks must also decide the role that Islam will play in the country's political life. Although Tajiks consider themselves part of the Islamic world, most citizens do not support the idea of making the country an Islamic state. Nevertheless, they do want to bring Islamic ideals into economic, educational, and social affairs.

Teahouses exist throughout Tajikistan. At these casual restaurants, patrons—usually men—sit cross-legged on raised, bedlike platforms. In addition to green tea, guests can order a light meal.

FAST FACTS ABOUT TAJIKISTAN

Total Population	5.5 million
Ethnic Mixture	62 percent Tajik 24 percent Uzbek 8 percent Russian 1.3 percent Kyrgyz 1.5 percent Tatar 1 percent German 1 percent Ukrainian
CAPITAL and Major Cities	DUSHANBE, Khojent, Panjikent, Kulyab, Kurgan-Tyube, Ura-Tyube
Major Languages	Tajik, Uzbek, Russian
Major Religion	Islam (Sunni branch)
Year of Inclusion in USSR	1929
Status	Independent nation; joined Commonwealth of Independent States in 1991; member of United Nations since 1992; armed clashes between pro-Islamic and pro-Communist factions

(Above) *Anti-Communist demonstrators continue to push for reforms in the new Tajik government, which changed leaders several times in 1992 and 1993.* (Below) *Amid the civil instability, daily life—including the making of traditional foods—continues.*

Another challenge to the Tajik leadership is the lack of ethnic Tajik managers, administrators, planners, and other professionals. Until the 1970s, Tajiks were excluded from high-level jobs because they did not speak Russian well. The Tajik government wants to train more Tajiks to manage the country's valuable hydroelectric, chemical, and machine-building industries.

Complicating this issue is the continuing emigration of ethnic Russians, who once represented a large portion of the skilled work force. The departure of teachers and doctors, for example, has slowed Tajikistan's improvements in education and health care. Although a Tajik labor surplus exists, time and money are needed to train unskilled workers.

Political instability is Tajikistan's biggest challenge. Unused to freedom and democracy, Tajiks may be wasting an opportunity to achieve a better standard of living. In addition, the ongoing violence threatens the cultural and religious traditions that survived more than 60 years of Communist control. Unless the factions in Tajikistan can come together, stability and progress will remain out of reach.

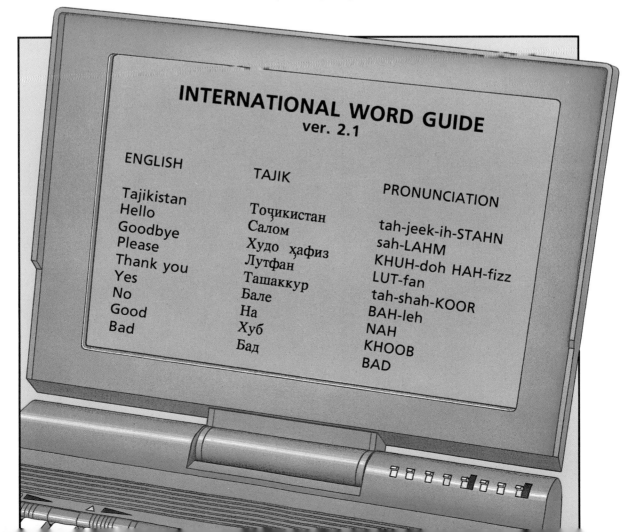

INTERNATIONAL WORD GUIDE
ver. 2.1

ENGLISH	TAJIK	PRONUNCIATION
Tajikistan	Тоҷикистан	tah-jeek-ih-STAHN
Hello	Салом	sah-LAHM
Goodbye	Худо ҳафиз	KHUH-doh HAH-fizz
Please	Лутфан	LUT-fan
Thank you	Ташаккур	tah-shah-KOOR
Yes	Бале	BAH-leh
No	На	NAH
Good	Хуб	KHOOB
Bad	Бад	BAD

• GLOSSARY •

afghanets: a dry wind that blows in southwestern Tajikistan.

collective farm: a large agricultural estate worked by a group. The workers usually received a portion of the farm's harvest as wages. On a Soviet collective farm, the central government owned the land, buildings, and machinery.

Commonwealth of Independent States: a union of former Soviet republics that was created by the leaders of Russia, Belarus, and Ukraine in December 1991. The commonwealth has no formal constitution and functions as a loose economic and military association.

Communist: a person who supports Communism—an economic system in which the government owns all farmland and the means of producing goods in factories.

Donkeys piled high with firewood make their way slowly down a mountain slope.

The interiors of many urban teahouses are often decorated with elaborate geometric designs.

coup d'état: French words meaning "blow to the state" that refer to a swift, sudden overthrow of a government.

delimitation: the process of defining the borders of a territory.

ethnic Russian: a person whose ethnic heritage is Slavic and who speaks Russian.

ethnic Tajik: a person whose ethnic heritage is Persian and who speaks Tajik.

ethnic Uzbek: a person whose ethnic heritage is Turkic and who speaks Uzbek.

garmsir: meaning "hot place" in Persian, a hot, dry wind that blows into Tajikistan from the south.

glasnost: the Russian word for openness that refers to a Soviet policy of easing restrictions on writing and speaking.

industrialize: to build and modernize factories for the purpose of manufacturing a wide variety of consumer goods and machinery.

khan: the leader of a central Asian domain, called a **khanate**, who ruled Turkic, Mongol, or Tatar peoples.

People's Republic of Bukhara: an early member of the Soviet Union that was eventually included in the lands of the Uzbek Soviet Socialist Republic.

perestroika: a policy of economic restructuring introduced in the late 1980s. Under perestroika, the Soviet state loosened its control of industry and agriculture and allowed small private businesses to operate.

protectorate: a self-governing territory under the protection and influence of a foreign power.

qishlaq: the Tajik word for a small village.

Russian Empire: a large kingdom ruled by czars that covered present-day Russia as well as areas to the west and south. It existed from roughly the mid-1500s to 1917.

Russian Turkestan: the western part of central Asia that the Russian Empire took over in the 19th century.

satrap: the governor of a region, called a **satrapy**, in the ancient Persian Empire.

Sharia: a collection of Islamic laws based on rules of conduct in the Koran.

Turkestan Autonomous Soviet Socialist Republic: an early member of the Soviet Union that was eventually divided into five separate republics, one of which was the Tajik Soviet Socialist Republic.

Turkize: to make Turkic by introducing the Turkic language and culture to non-Turkic peoples.

Union of Soviet Socialist Republics (USSR): a large nation in eastern Europe and northern Asia that consisted of 15 member-republics. It existed from 1922 to 1991.

United Nations: an international organization formed after World War II whose primary purpose is to promote world peace through discussion and cooperation.

Zoroastrianism: an ancient Persian religion that was founded in about the 6th century B.C.

About 4 percent of Tajiks live to be older than 65 years of age.

Kebabs—skewered chunks of lamb—are popular meat dishes at restaurants, at streetside stalls, and in homes.

• *Photo Acknowledgments* •

Photographs are used courtesy of: pp. 1, 19 (bottom left), 35 (bottom), 42, 53, Patty Winpenny; pp. 2, 5, 17 (top), 19 (bottom right), © Mary Ann Brockman; pp. 6, 21, 40, 47 (bottom), 50 (bottom), © Jim Richardson; p. 8, NOVOSTI/SOVFOTO; pp. 9 (left), 12 (right), 16 (top), 18 (bottom), 20 (bottom), 22 (left), 33 (left), 39, 43 (right), 45 (left), 52, © Yury Tatarinov; pp. 9 (right), 38 (bottom), 50 (top), ITAR-TASS/SOVFOTO; pp. 10, 26, 37, 47 (top), 54, Naomi Duguid/Asia Access; pp. 12 (left), 24, 25 (right), 30, Nasrin Mirsaidi; p. 13, RIA-NOVOSTI/SOVFOTO; p. 16 (bottom), Lunar and Planetary Institute; pp. 17 (bottom), 20 (top), 25 (left), 38 (top), 48, TROPIX/ J. Lee; pp. 18 (top), 22 (right), TASS/SOVFOTO; p. 19 (top), Steve Feinstein; pp. 23, 46 (bottom), 55, Intourist; p. 28, James H. Marrinan; p. 31, © Tim Riley; p. 32, James Ford Bell Library, University of Minnesota; p. 33 (right), Metropolitan Museum of Art, Cora Timken Burnett Collection of Persian Miniatures and Other Persian Art Objects, Bequest of Cora Timken Burnett, 1956; p. 35 (top), National Army Museum, London; pp. 36 (top), 46 (top), Michael Hamburger; p. 36 (bottom), G. S. Verkhonskiy/Erfan Publications; pp. 43 (left), 45 (right), © Robert Holmes. Maps and charts: pp. 14-15, 44, J. Michael Roy; pp. 28-29, 50, 51, Laura Westlund.

Covers: (Front and Back) © Yury Tatarinov